It's Easy To Play Showtunes.

Wise Publications
London/New York/Sydney/Cologne

Exclusive distributors:
Music Sales Limited
78 Newman Street, London W1P 3LA, England
Music Sales Pty. Limited
27 Clarendon Street, Artarmon, Sydney, NSW 2064, Australia

Cover illustration by Phil Dobson
Compilation by Peter Evans
Arranger Cyril Watters

This book © Copyright 1980 by
Wise Publications
ISBN 0.86001.776.1
Order No. AM 26907

Music Sales complete catalogue lists thousands
of titles and is free from your local music
book shop, or direct from Music Sales Limited.
Please send 25p in stamps for postage to
Music Sales Limited, 78 Newman Street, London W1P 3LA.

Printed in England by
West Central Printing Co. Limited, London and Suffolk.

3'50

Cabaret

(From the Motion Picture "Cabaret")

Music by John Kander
Lyrics by Fred Ebb

Moderate tempo

f

F6   C7+

1. What good   is   sit-ting   a - lone in your   room?
2. Put down   the   knit-ting,   the   book and the   broom,

mf

F   F+   F   C7+

Come hear   the   mu - sic   play;
Time for   a   hol - i -   day;

F   Fmaj7   F7   E♭   F

Life   is   a   Cab - a -   ret, old   chum,

B♭   Fdim   Am   Cm6 Cdim D7

way. _____
stay. _____

Cm7   F7   Eb F Bb   Fdim

- ret, old   chum, ____   Come to   the   cab - a - ret. ____

Am7   D7   Gm7   Bb   F

____   Come taste the   - ret, old   chum, ____

(no chord)   Am   Cm6 Cdim D7   Gm D7

On - ly   a   cab - a - ret, old chum, ____   So   come to

Bb   Fdim   Am7   D7   A7   Gm7

____   the   cab - a - ret. _____   sfz

F

Sunrise Sunset
(From the Musical "Fiddler On The Roof")
Words by Sheldon Harnick
Music by Jerry Bock

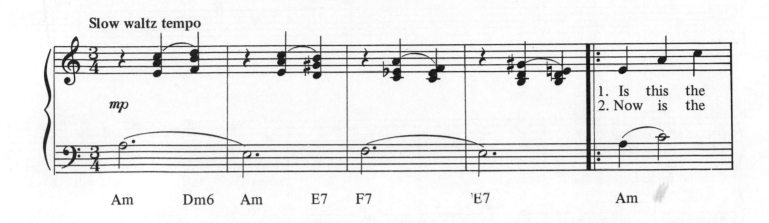

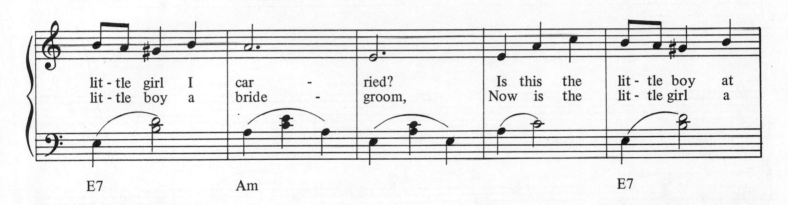

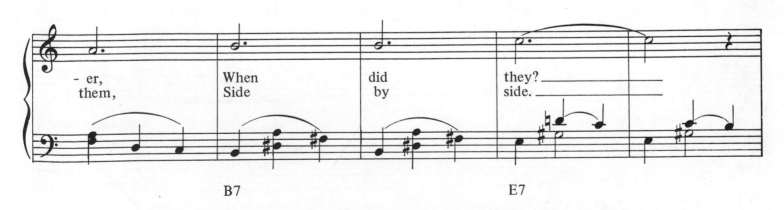

ov-er-night to sun - flow'rs, Bloss-om-ing ev-en as we

G7   C   Am   Dm6   E7

gaze. Sun - rise, sun - set, sun - rise,

Am   Am   Dm6   Am E7   Am   Dm6

sun - set, Swift-ly fly the years;

Am E7   Am   Dm6   Am Dm6   Am   A7

One sea - son fol-low-ing an-oth - er, La - den with

Dm   Ddim   Am7   D7   Dm6

hap-pi-ness and tears. tears.
ritard.

E7   Am   Am

As Long As He Needs Me

(From the Motion Picture "Oliver")

Words & Music by Lionel Bart

strong, _____ As long as he needs me. _____ If you are

G7 **Fm6** **G7** **Cmaj7** **C6**

lone - ly, _____ then you will know _____ When some-one needs you, _____ you love them

Bb6 F **G7** **C6** **Dm6 Am D7**

so. _____ I won't be - tray his trust, _____ Tho' peo-ple

Dm7 **G7** **Cmaj7** **C6** **Cmaj7** **C6**

say I must. I've got to stay true, just _____ As long as

Cmaj7 C#dim **Dm7** **G7** **Dm** **D9**

1

he needs me. _____ As long as

2

he needs me. _____

ritard.

Dm7 **G7** **C** **Dm7** **G7(b9) C6**

11

What Kind of Fool Am I

(From the Musical "Stop The World I Want to Get Off")

Words & Music by Leslie Bricusse & Anthony Newley

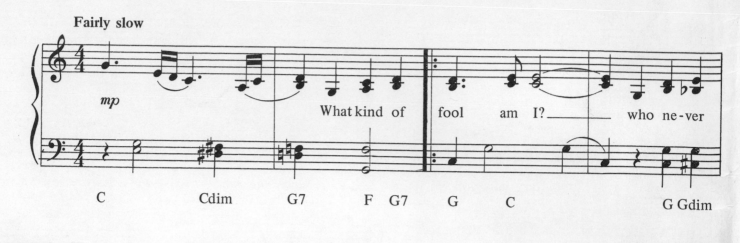

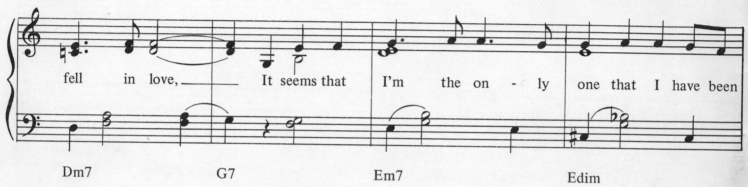

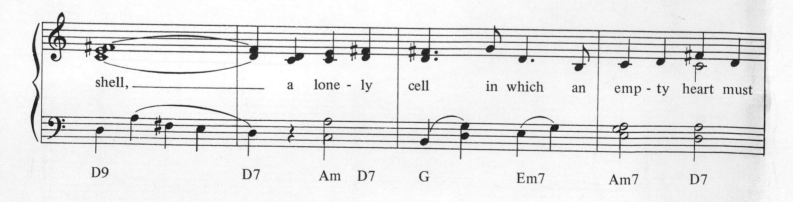

dwell. _____ What kind of lips are these, _____ that lied with
What kind of clown am I? _____ What do I

Dm7   G7   F   G7   G   C   G   Gdim

ev - 'ry kiss? _____ That whis-pered emp - ty words of love that left me a-
know of life? _____ Why can't I cast a - way the mask of play and

Dm7   G7   Em7   Gm6

lone like this. _____ Why can't I fall in love _____ like an - y
live my life? _____ Why can't I fall in love _____ till I don't

A7   Gm6   A7   (no chord)   F   Bb7

oth - er man? _____ And may - be then I'll know what kind of fool I
give a damn? _____

C   D7   Dm7   Fm6

1
am.   What kind of

C   A7   Dm7   F   G7

2
am.   *mf*
ritard.

C   Ab Bb   C

13

Stranger In Paradise

(From the Musical "Kismet")

Words & Music by Robert Wright & George Forrest

Take my hand,____ I'm a stran-ger in par-a-dise,

All lost in a won-der-land, a stran-ger in par-a-dise.

If I stand star-ry eyed,____ That's a dan-ger in par-a-dise,

For mor-tals who stand be-side / An an-gel like you.

F   Gm7   C7(♭9)   F

I saw your face _____ and I as-cend-ed _____

(no chord)   D♭7   C♭ D♭7 D♭   G♭

_____ Out of the com-mon-place _____ in-to the rare!

Eb m6   F7   B♭m

Some-where in space _____ I hang sus-pend-ed,

A7   G A7 Dmaj7 D6

_____ Un-til I know _____ there's a chance that you care. _____

Gm7   C7   F

Won't you ans-wer the fer-vent prayer ___ of a stran-ger in

Cdim   Gm7   C7

par - a-dise?   Don't send me in   dark des - pair   From all that I

Fmaj7   F   Gm7   C7(♭9)

hun-ger for;   But o - pen your   an - gel's arms   To the stran-ger in

F   G7   C7

par - a-dise.   And tell {him/her} that {he/she} need be   a stran-ger no

Am   F   D7   Gm7   C7(♭9)

more. ___   *ritard.*

F   E♭m7   F

Consider Yourself

(From the Motion Picture "Oliver")
Words & Music by Lionel Bart

Con - sid - er your self _____ our mate, _____

G7   G7+   C   G7   C

We don't want to have _____ no fuss. _____

A7   Dm   A7+   Dm

For aft - er some con - sid - er - a - tion, we can

B   C   Gm6

state: Con - sid - er your - self _____

A7   Dm

f one of us. _____

G7   C   no chord

Maybe This Time
(From the Motion Picture "Cabaret")
Music by John Kander
Lyrics by Fred Ebb

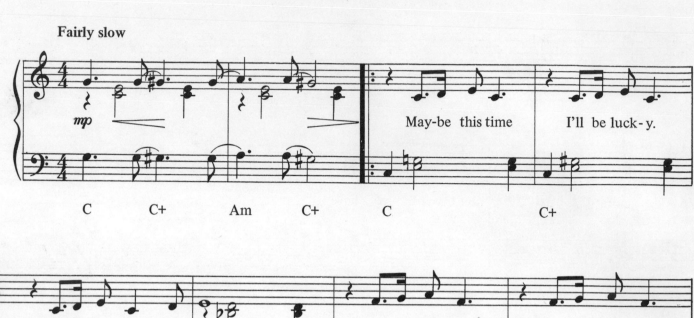

time be-fore.___ Ev-'ry-bo-dy loves a win-ner, so no-bo-dy loved

D7   F G   C   C+   Am

me.   La- dy Peaceful,   La-dy Hap-py,   That's what I long to   be.

C7   F   F+   Dm   Adim

All the odds are   in my fav - our,   some-thing's bound to be-gin.

G7   Am   D7

1

It's got to hap-pen,   hap-pen some-time;   May-be this time I'll win.

C   C+   Dm7   C

2

May-be this time,   May-be this time I'll   win.___   *ritard.*

Am   Dm7   C

On The Street Where You Live

(From the Musical "My Fair Lady")

Words by Alan Jay Lerner
Music by Frederick Loewe

Let The Sunshine In

(From the Musical "Hair")

Words by James Rado & Gerome Ragni
Music by Galt MacDermot

Fairly slow

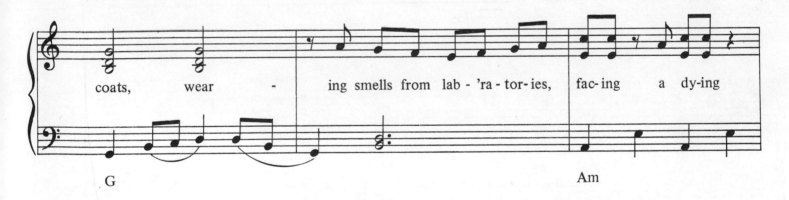

lies   with su‑ preme vis‑ions of lone‑ly tunes.   Some ‑ where,

Am   F   C   Am

in ‑ side some ‑thing, there is a rush   of   great‑ness, Who knows what stands in

front   of   our lives; I fash ‑ion my___ fu ‑ture   on films in space.

G   Am   C

Si ‑ lence tells me   se‑cret ‑ ly   ev ‑ ’ry‑thing.___

Am   E7   Am

Ev ‑   ’ry ‑ thing.   Sing ‑   ing

Fmaj7   F6   C   Am

Ain't Misbehavin'
(From the Musical "Ain't Misbehavin")
Words by Andy Razaf
Music by Thomas Waller & Harry Brooks

I'm sav-in' my love for you. Like Jack Hor-ner,

Dm G7 C C7 F7 E7 Am

in the cor-ner, don't go no-where, what do I care? Your kiss-es

F7 D7 A7 G Bm6 Ddim

are worth wait-in' for, be - lieve me. I don't stay out late,

Am D7 G7 A7 D9 G7 C

don't care to go, I'm home a-bout eight, just me and my ra-di-o, Ain't mis-be-hav-in',

Dm G9 C E7 F6 Fm C Eb7

1
2

I'm sav-in' my love for you.

Dm G7 C F6 C G7 C

I Remember It Well

(From the Motion Picture "Gigi")

Words by Alan Jay Lerner
Music by Frederick Loewe

yes! I re - mem - ber it well. That
yes! I re - mem - ber it well. You

Gm   C7   F

dazz - ling A - pril moon! (She) There was none that night,
wore a gown of gold. I was all in blue.

Bb   Bb+   Gm   Bbm

(She) And the month was June! (He) That's right! That's right! (She) It warms my
(He) Am I get - ting old? (She) Oh no! Not you! How strong you

F   Ab   Cm D7   Gm7   C7

heart to know that you re - mem - ber still the way you do. (He) {Ah
were, how young and gay; A prince of love in ev - 'ry way. {Ah

F   F7   Bb

yes! I re - mem - ber it well. *mf*
yes! I re - mem - ber it well.

F   C7   F6

I'll Never Fall In Love Again

(From the Musical "Promises, Promises")
Words by Hal David
Music by Burt Bacharach

Steady four

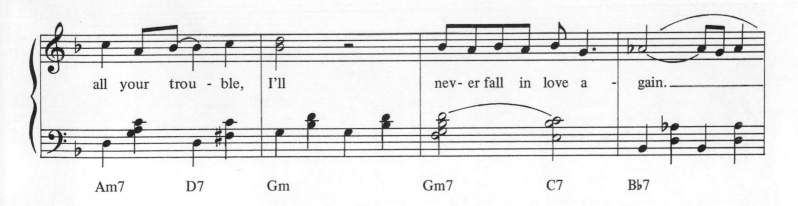

What do you get when you kiss a {guy,___ / girl,___} You get e-nough germs to
What do you get when you give your heart,___ You get it all bro-ken
What do you get when you need a {girl,___ / guy,___} You get e-nough tears to

F   Dm   Bb

catch pneu - mo - nia,   Af - ter you do, she'll   nev - er   phone you;   I'll
up and   bat - tered,   That's what you get,   a   heart that's shat - tered;   I'll
fill an   o - cean,   That's what you get   for   your de - vo - tion;

Am7   Am7   D7   Gm

nev-er fall in love a - gain.___   I'll   nev - er fall in love a -

Gm7   C7   Bb7   F   Bbmaj7   C7

gain.   Don't tell me what it's all   a -

F   Fmaj7   F   Fmaj7   F   Dm   Gm7

bout,   'Cause   I've been there, and I'm   glad I'm out;___   Out of those chains, those

F   Gm7   F   Am

34

chains that bind ___ you, That is why I'm here to re-mind you. What do you get when you

G7   C   C7   F

fall in love, ___ You on-ly get lies and pain and sor-row,

Dm   B♭

So for at least un-til to-mor-row, I'll nev-er fall in love a-

Am7   D7   Gm   Gm7   C7

1

gain. ___ I'll nev-er fall in love a - gain.

B♭7   F   B♭maj7   C7   B♭ C7   F   Fmaj7

2

nev-er fall in love a - gain.

ritard   *a tempo*

F   Fmaj7   C7   B♭ C7   F   Fmaj7   F

Hello Dolly

(From the Motion Picture "Hello Dolly")

Words & Music by Jerry Herman

go - in' strong. We feel the room   sway - in', for the

C6   Cdim   G7   C

band's   play - in' one of   your old fav - 'rite   songs from 'way back

Am   Gm7   C7   Gm7   C7

when.   So,   { take her   wrap, fel - las,   Find her an emp - ty
                      { gol - ly   gee, fel - las,   Find her a vac - ant

Am7 Dm   Dm6   E7   Am   Em   Am

lap,   fel - las,}   Dol - ly 'll nev - er   go a - way a - gain!   Hel -
knee,   fel - las,}

Em   D9   F   G7   C   A7   Dm   G7

go a - way.   Dol - ly 'll nev - er   go a - way a - gain!   sfz

F   G7   D9   F   G7   C

Aquarius
(From the Musical "Hair")

Words by James Rado & Gerome Ragni
Music by Galt MacDermot

love will steer the stars. This is the dawn - ing of the

F   G7   C (no chord)

age of A - quar - i - us, The age of A - quar - i - us,

Bb

A - quar - i - us,

Dm   F   G7

A - quar - i - us,

Dm

FINE

Har-mo-ny and un-der - stand-ing, Sym-pa-thy and trust a - bound - ing.

C7   F   C7   F

No more false- hoods or de - ri -sions, Gold - en liv -ing dreams of vi -sions, Mys-tic

C7   F   Dm   Gdim   F

crys - tal rev - e - la - tion, And the mind's true lib - er - a - tion. A -

A7   Dm   Dm7   Gm   F

quar - i - us, _____ A -

Gm7   Gm

D.S. al FINE

quar - i - us. _____ When the

Dm

40

Day By Day

(From the Musical "Godspell")

Music by Stephen Schwartz
Lyrics by John Michael Tebelak

Moderate waltz tempo

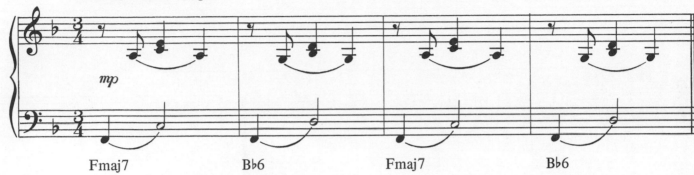

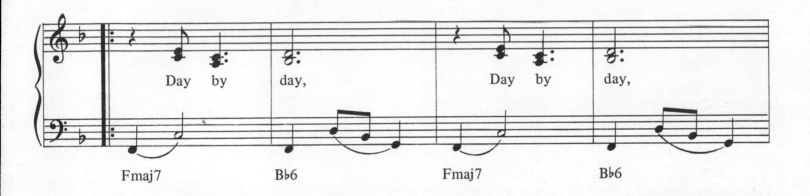

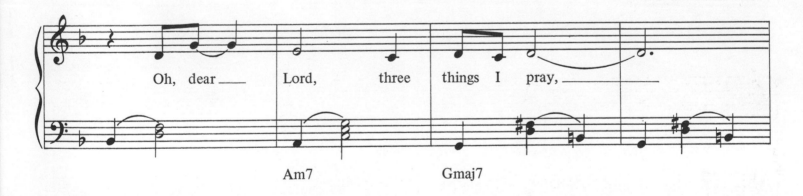

If I Were A Rich Man

(From the Motion Picture "Fiddler On The Roof")

Words by Sheldon Harnick
Music by Jerry Bock

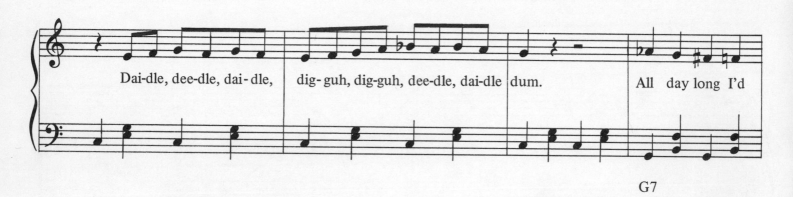

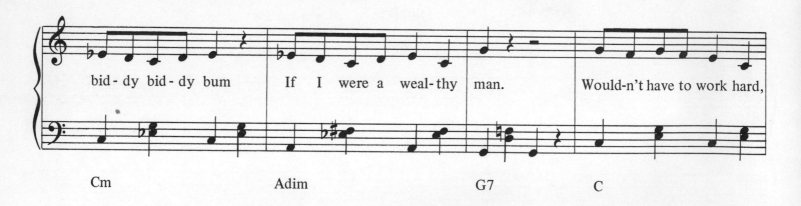

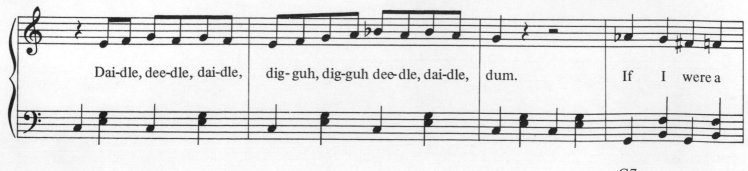

Quasi rubato

bid - dy, bid - dy rich,   dig - guh, dig - guh, dee - dle, daidle man. {1. I'd build a / 2. I see my}   big tall house with / wife, my Gold - e,

Cm   Adim   G7   C (no chord)   Fm7

rooms by the do - zen, / looking like a rich man's   Right in the mid - dle of the / wife with a pro - per dou - ble   town; / chin;   A / I   fine tin roof with / Su - per - vis - ing

Bb7   Ebmaj7   Bbm   C7   Fm

real woo - den floors be - low. / meals to her heart's de - light.   There could be / I see her   one long stair - case / putting on airs and

G7   C   C7   Bb   C7   Fm7

just go - ing up and / strutting like a pea - cock,   one ev - en long - er com - ing / Oy! what a hap - py mood she's   down; / in.   And / Scream - ing at the   one more lead - ing

Bb7   Ebmaj7   Bb6   C7   Fm

To Coda ⊕

no - where just for / ser - vants day and   show. _____ / night. _____   I'd fill my   yard with chicks and

F#dim   G   Cm6   G   Bb   C7   F

tur - keys and geese And ducks for the town to see and hear;

C   Gm   A7

Squawk-ing just as nois - i - ly as they can.   And each loud

Dm   F+ Dm7 G7   C   C7   Bb C7

quack and cluck and gob-ble and honk will land like a trum-pet in the ear;   As

Fm   Fm7   Bb7   Ebmaj7   Bbm   C7

D.%. al Coda

if to say here lives a wealth-y man. _____   (Sigh)

Fm   F#dim   G   Cm6   G   G7

⊕ CODA

(sigh) If I were a rich man, Dai-dle dee-dle, daidle, dig-guh, dig-guh, deedle, daidle,

46   G   G7   C

dum. All day long I'd bid-dy bid-dy bum If I were a weal-thy

G7   Cm   Adim

man. Would-n't have to work hard, Dai-dle, dee-dle, dai-dle,

G7   C

dig - guh, dig - guh, dee-dle, dai - dle, dum. Lord, who made the

Rubato

G7

li - on and the lamb, You de-creed I should be what I am, Would it spoil some

Cm   G7   Cm   G7

vast e - ter-nal plan, If I were a weal - thy man? _____

Cm   Adim   G7   C   G   C